Photography by John Baker

The publisher wishes to thank Rosabelle
Needham and Honey Pendrous for their
help in producing this book, and A–Z
Botanical Collection Limited for supplying
some of the photographs.

Published 1979 by The Hamlyn Publishing Group Limited
London . New York . Sydney . Toronto
Astronaut House, Feltham, Middlesex, England
Designed and produced for The Hamlyn Publishing Group Limited
by Asset Publishing Limited
Copyright © 1979 Asset Publishing Limited
ISBN 0 600 32988 7   Printed in Italy

Country Crafts
Dried Flowers
Olive Odell

Hamlyn
London·New York·Sydney·Toronto

Contents

Practically all fresh flowers have a short life, and if you have to buy them it can be an expensive one too. However, by planning and thinking ahead, a more or less permanent collection of dried and preserved floral 'material' can be collected. Properly stored, most of this material will keep for years, giving

Even if you do not have a garden of your own, the range of wild flowers, grasses, seed heads and leaves available for picking in country hedgerows, is enormous. Do remember, though, that some plants are becoming increasingly rare, so pick from a well-established plant or tree and if you have any doubts about possible ownership, ask permission.

Many florists stock a wide range of dried material which, although expensive, can help to form the basis of a collection. Friends with gardens can be another source of help. Try growing grasses and cereals for drying in a window box or a large flower pot on the

Introduction

window ledge. A good pinch of cage bird seed planted indoors in a pot, or outside in a corner of the garden, will provide some interesting grasses for easy drying.

There are several methods of preserving plant material; it is fun to try them all, but choose those which suit the space and facilities available. When drying or preserving, select the best of what is available, and as a general rule, pick before full maturity. Flowers that are full grown or 'overblown' (i.e. those that are really past their prime) will fade rapidly and disintegrate quickly. Always cut flowers and plant material on a dry, warm day, *never* when it is raining or after the dew has fallen. The reason for this is that material picked wet, or even damp, is liable to become mildewed during the drying or preserving process. Many flowers will lose some of their original bright colours, these being replaced by more subtle and delicate colouring. Leaves preserved by the glycerine method (see page 14), will provide a wonderful variation of colours from creams to deep brown, depending upon the type of leaves and whether they are stored in dark or light conditions. Green or grey leaves can be produced by pressing or drying in a desiccant such as silica gel or borax (see page 12).

As well as providing all corners of your home with attractive and long-lasting arrangements of all shapes and sizes, there are many other ways in which dried and preserved material can be used. Bookmarks, Christmas or gift cards and tags, calendars, miniature bell pulls, pictures, plaques, posies and flower balls are just a few of the things you can make. Much of the fun and pleasure in using dried materials comes from experimenting with your own ideas to find new combinations of colour, texture and design and original things to make.

Methods of preservation

Air-drying

This is the simplest of all methods of drying and requires no sophisticated equipment as the material is merely left to dry naturally. All you need is an airy space with room for hooks or to string a line from which you can hang the flowers, grasses or whatever.

If possible, choose a cool, dry, dark and airy place to hang the material. Too much light and warmth can produce faded and brittle results, while a damp atmosphere may cause mildew.

If space is very limited, use wire coat hangers, tie the bunches of flowers etc. to the lower rung, and then hook the hangers over the line.

The most important factor in this method of drying is to allow enough space for the air to circulate round *each* flower or seed head. For this reason, it is often better to hang large flower heads separately, tying only smaller flowers into small bunches.

Pick the material you want to dry, remove the leaves from the stems, then tie the stems together near the bottom with string, leaving a loop for hanging. As the material dries, it will shrink slightly, so check the ties during the drying period to make sure they are

Below: Beams in a loft or barn are an ideal place for hanging plant material to dry.

Above: Wired helichrysum heads dry quickly when stuck into a block of foam. Allow room for air to circulate between blooms.

holding the stems securely. Anything with very heavy or very fragile heads can be air-dried by standing upright in a container, but the plant must have a strong enough stem to support the head so it does not droop. If the stems of the flowers are short, cut them down still further so they are approximately 2·5 cm (1 in) from the head. Do this immediately after picking and push a length of

florist's wire up the stem and into the flower head, taking care not to penetrate through the centre. Push the wires into a pot of sand or a block of oasis to dry. As the flower dries, it will shrink and grip the wire tightly.

Alternatively, you can dry such wired blooms in a 'tray', which may be simply made by stretching a piece of 1 cm (½ in) chicken wire across the top of a box. Nail or staple the sides to keep the chicken wire in place, then drop the wire 'stems' through the holes. The heads will be supported whilst drying, so helping to keep them a good shape.

9

Hydrangeas (see opposite), acanthus and moluccella (bells of Ireland) can all be hung up and left to dry, but they require a little extra treatment beforehand. Cut the blooms as required in early autumn and strip off the leaves. Put the stems in a container holding about 5 cm (2 in) of water and leave in a warm room until the water has all been taken up by the flowers – this can be anything between seven to ten days. Then hang and dry in the usual way. Hydrangeas cut on a new stem will give the best results.

The length of drying time will vary; material such as delicate grasses may only take a week, while heavier material, containing a greater quantity of moisture, may need three to four weeks. Check occasionally to see how they are getting along.

Left: Hydrangeas and other woody-stemmed flowers are left to soak up a small amount of water before drying.

Below: The stems of grasses dried by standing them in a jam jar droop to give a variety of interesting shapes.

You can air-dry grasses by standing them upright (without water) in a container such as a jam jar. Instead of the straight, stiff stems produced by tying in bunches and hanging upside down, this method results in much more pliable and less rigid stems, which can be useful for giving a curved effect to the sides of an arrangement, for example. Try drying grasses by both these methods – all results will be useful.

The true everlasting flowers (see guide) are the easiest of all flowers to dry, and will virtually dry on the stalk if you let them, although it is better to pick them before they do this. They all have a papery texture and are easy to grow. You will find they last longer and dry better if you grow them in the sunniest part of the garden, and they are also at their best for drying after a dry summer. Cut them before the outside petals can be easily pulled away, with as long a stem as possible. As a general rule, however, all everlasting flowers need to be wired or given a false stem if they are to be used in an arrangement. They can be put in a box in a warm place and left to finish drying naturally.

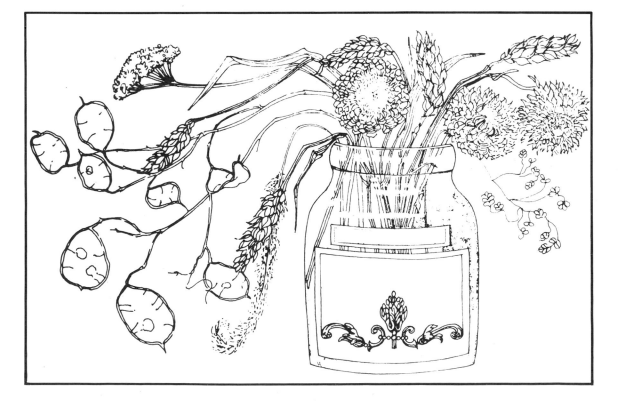

Drying with desiccant powder

The principle of this method of drying is to use a desiccant powder which absorbs all the moisture from the plant material, leaving it completely dry.

If space is a problem this is a useful method, as all that is required is a large box to hold the powder and the flowers. Borax, silica gel, alum or sand can all be used and flowers preserved by this method keep much of their true original colour, although they do tend to be very delicate. The open-faced flowers are usually the most successful, but experiment with others too – I have seen dahlias, roses and lilies in superb condition after this method of drying. Clear red and orange roses keep their colour well, wild gentians and sprigs of delphinium are also worth trying as their beautiful blue colour is preserved.

Below: When using dessicant powder, the flower heads should not touch one another.

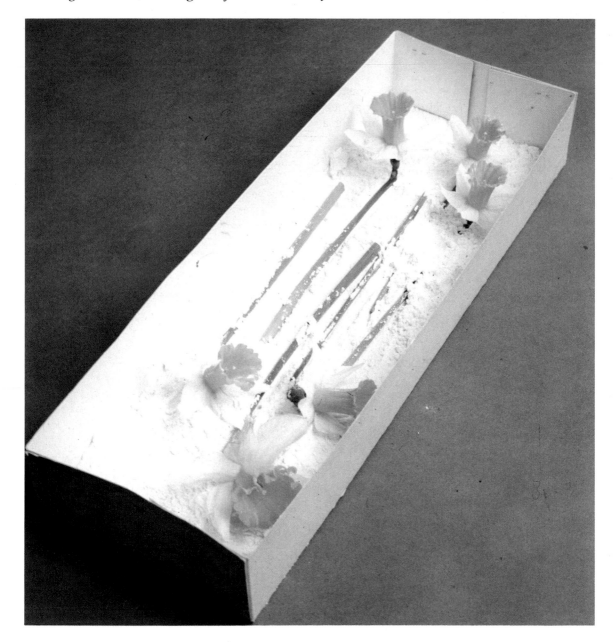

Borax, silica gel and alum can be bought at most chemists and all these powders can be used time and again, provided they are kept in a dry place until required and sieved occasionally. Fine, dry, clean sand can be used, but may be too heavy for delicate flowers.

Pick the flowers when they are absolutely dry and select only those in really prime condition. Choose a shallow box or tin of suitable size, cover the base with a layer of the powder you are using and lay the flowers on this. Cover them completely with more of the powder, making sure too that there is a good layer between all the separate petals and stamens. Put the box in a warm, dry place, preferably somewhere with even, constant warmth such as an airing cupboard or a shelf above the radiator, then leave it alone for a week or so, before checking.

As well as being a space-saving method of drying, this is also often considered to be the best method for preserving natural colours and contours of brightly-coloured, slightly more complex-shaped flowers.

It is better not to mix varieties of flowers in a drying tray if possible as some will take a longer time than others to dry, and the less disturbance they have during the drying process the better.

If you are using sand as a drying agent, silver sand is the best type to use as it is very fine and will filter down amongst the petals without crushing them. Fine river sand *can* be used, but it needs to be washed and thoroughly dried before use. In fact all sand should be dried before using; even if it feels dry, it may not be so.

To dry sand, put it in shallow tins in a low oven, 130°C, 250°F or Gas Mark $\frac{1}{2}$ for about 2–4 hours. Agitate it occasionally so that the heat penetrates right through it, and let it get completely cold before using it.

If you have none of the desiccants to hand, you can use salt or powdered starch, although starch will tend to cling to the petals a little. Remove any that remains after drying by brushing with a small, fine, paint brush.

The best desiccant is generally considered to be silica gel, which is obtainable in both powdered and granular form. It can absorb up to 50 per cent of its weight in water, which is rather more than the other desiccants. It also dries out the hands, so use rubber gloves when you are using it. Sieve it occasionally to break up any lumps and to remove broken petals, and dry it after use in the same way as sand.

Below: Cover blooms completely with powder.

The length of time it takes for the powder to draw the moisture from the petals will vary according to the size of the flower. Small flowers, such as pansies or violas, take only about two days, while roses or similar more complex flowers will take six to eight days. Test to see if the blooms are dry by very gently removing powder from a petal; if there is the slightest trace of moisture remaining, re-cover with the desiccant and leave a little longer.

When the flowers are quite dry, store them in a box in a dark, dry place, adding a few grains of silica gel or borax to absorb any moisture. If florist's wire is required to support the stems, it should be added before the drying process commences, so that it is held securely in place. The dried results will be too fragile to push wire through.

Preserving in glycerine

In general, this method of preservation is most suitable for sprays of foliage of varying types. Some flowers and seed heads can also be treated in this way (see under individual species in guide). The principle involved is that the water in the plants is replaced by glycerine, to produce a long-lasting material, which is generally considerably more supple and pliant than dried material. It is in fact a method of *preservation* rather than drying.

As with other methods of drying or preservation, it is advisable to choose material in good condition. Split any stems that are particularly woody, so the glycerine can travel up them more easily. Then stand the spray in water for a few hours – this has the effect of 'freshening' it. The process of taking water up the stem also encourages it to do the same once it is put in the glycerine.

Mix together one part glycerine to two parts boiling water (hot water mixes with glycerine more easily than cold) and leave to cool. Put the glycerine solution into a narrow, deep container (which is capable of supporting the stems and branches you want to preserve) to a depth of about 10 cm (4 in). Stand the sprays in it and leave them to absorb the solution.

The length of time the plant takes to absorb sufficient glycerine to preserve it, which means the solution must go right to the tip of the leaves, depends on individual species and at what stage of life they have been picked. It can actually vary from two days to three weeks, during which time the leaves change from shades of golden brown to rich mahogany. Check the container regularly; if you look at the backs of the leaves, you can often see the glycerine mixture creeping along the veins, and so can detect when it reaches the top. Test the leaves between your finger and thumb (leaves should be supple, but not oily) and remove them from the mixture if they appear to be ready. If after removal from the mixture leaves do begin to droop, hang them upside down for a couple of days to encourage the glycerine to reach the top. Otherwise, just dab them dry with a soft cloth and either lay them between paper in suitably sized boxes, or keep them carefully in *perforated* polythene bags. Keep in a dry place in a moderate temperature where they are not likely to be crushed by some heavy object.

Gather material to be preserved by this method before late autumn colours begin to show. If you pick them *after* the sap has stopped rising during growth, the plant will not be able to absorb the liquid glycerine solution. In damp seasons, when growth has been wet and 'soft', the leaves may not absorb the glycerine mixture, so be prepared for

occasional failures.

Preserving by pressing

For the purpose of this book, we are not referring here to heavy pressing to make the material completely flat and fragile, suitable for sticking down on to card or in books, etc. Instead it refers to a 'light' pressing of specially selected plant items, which can then be used in free-standing arrangements. Ferns and leaves are easily preserved by this method; they retain their shape well, although the stems of leaves will automatically

flatten, and lose a little of their natural 'bounce'. Besides ferns try small sprays of beech, horse chestnut, sycamore, maple and oak. The leaves of hosta, bergenia, iris and crocosmia all press well too.

Pick the material when it is dry and in good condition and lay it flat between sheets of newspaper. Slide these carefully under the carpet in a room that receives regular 'traffic' across it. Alternatively you can put the 'sandwich' of newspaper and leaves or ferns between the pages of a thick book, such as an old telephone directory, and then put a good heavy weight – an iron or a brick for example – on top. Check the material after seven days; ferns, when ready, will feel dry and papery, but still have some 'three-dimensional' shape. They may also have changed colour slightly. Store any material preserved in this way in boxes and keep in a dry place.

A very simple method of 'instant pressing' which is worth trying is to place the leaves between several thicknesses of newspaper and iron gently with a cool iron (set at 'wool'). Try experimenting with the early autumn-coloured leaves. Don't expect material treated in this way to last as long as the other preservation methods. Six to eight weeks is the maximum life, but it can be ideal for an 'instant' arrangement.

Evergreens need a slightly different treatment if you want to press them. After picking, wash the sprays gently in lukewarm water, rinse them, and shake gently to remove surplus water. When they are dry lay them between sheets of newspaper, and pile these on top of each other, putting extra sheets of newspaper between the layers. Top the pile with a piece of thin cardboard, tie the whole bundle into a parcel and place a light weight on top. Leave in a dry, warm place for approximately four weeks, by which time they should be dry. With this method, the leaves and branches retain more of their natural 'bounce'.

Left: Some leaves and ferns lend themselves well to drying by gentle pressing.

15

Special preservation methods

Ivy leaves, either as individual leaves or in a trailing 'spray', will keep well for many months if you paint them all over with clear varnish. Try this also with the sword-shaped iris leaves. Many evergreens, such as spruce, bay and plain and variegated holly, will dry on their own, although they may have a shorter life than other preserved materials. Just wash them gently in lukewarm water, shake dry, then hang in bunches to dry or leave upright in jam jars.

Reed mace also require specialized treatment to preserve them. Cut them when the head is a soft brown colour and velvety to touch. Mix 600 ml (1 pint) methylated spirit

Above: Try various methods of preservation on sprigs of foliage to achieve a variety of effects. It is best to try such experiments on hardy evergreens. Protect your working surface in case of spillage or staining.

and 25 g (1 oz) of 'shellac', and leave it to stand for 72 hours. Stir well before use, then dip the mace heads into the mixture and leave them for ten minutes. Remove from mixture and stand upright in a jar, so they dry off naturally. With careful storage and handling, once treated this way, there is no reason at all why they should not keep in good condition for years.

Storage

The lidded cardboard boxes in which florists receive flowers from the markets are excellent for storing dried material and florists can usually be persuaded to part with them. Keep foliage and flowers separately, if at all possible, and put the flatter material, such as ferns, at the base of the box with the other material on top.

The drying 'trays' mentioned on page 13 can also be used for storing plant material, while plastic or polythene boxes, such as those used in freezers or refrigerators, are useful for storing acorns, nuts, cones and smaller flowers such as individual bells of Ireland. Grasses, wheat, barley and the like will keep perfectly well standing in a jam jar or similar container, which must, of course, be deep enough to support the stalks.

Most preserved or dried plant material, if stored in the right conditions – i.e. away from damp and excessive heat or light – should last for several years. It should always be handled with care, particularly the more fragile and delicate material, and the boxes and containers should not be crushed or over-crowded. When not in continuous use check the condition occasionally, and do not be disappointed at the odd failure. Be prepared to throw out a few things as they get tired and tatty – after all, you will probably be adding to your stock each year. Use a small, soft, artist's paint brush for removing any dust.

Preserved foliage which may have become a little 'flat' and tired-looking after a bout in storage, can sometimes be freshened by holding it over a steaming kettle for a while. Large preserved leaves can also be curled (if you want this effect in an arrangement) by holding them over steam for a few minutes and, while they are still pliable, gently stroking and bending them into the required shape. If necessary, clip them in position with hair grips or tie them in place while the leaf dries out after steaming.

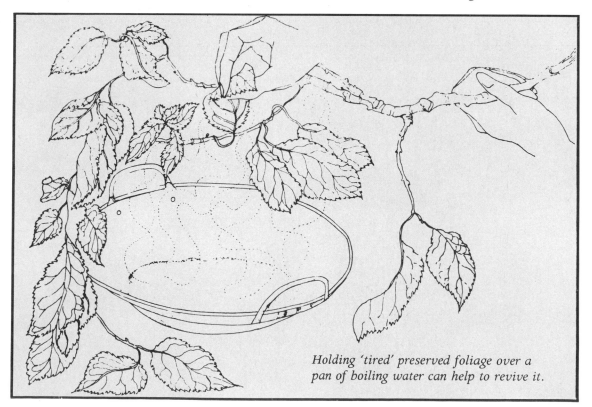

Holding 'tired' preserved foliage over a pan of boiling water can help to revive it.

A guide to plant material

Classification	Plant material	Method of preservation
Acacia dealbata (Mimosa)	This native of Australia can be grown in greenhouse but is more usually bought fresh from florists in spring. The yellow flowerballs will shrink a little during drying.	Dry naturally by hanging in bunches.
Acanthus (Bear's Breeches)	Herbaceous, easy-to-grow perennial. Spikes of purple or white flowers grow 60–90 cm (2–3 ft) high in summer and are excellent for large arrangements.	Dry naturally by hanging individually from a line.
Achillea filipendulina (Garden Yarrow)	Herbaceous, easy-to-grow perennial with 90–150 cm (3–5 ft) stems carrying flat heads of deep yellow. 'Gold Plate' and 'Coronation Gold' are two excellent varieties for drying. Pick in early to mid-summer before flowers start to discolour round the edges.	Stand stems in 5 cm (2 in) water. When this is absorbed, hang upside down in bunches.
Amaranthus (Love-lies-bleeding)	Half-hardy annual, with tassels or 'racemes' of crimson flowers up to 45 cm (18 in) long. Flowers from summer to autumn. Pick it for drying in summer, when stems have turned crimson.	Dry naturally by hanging in bunches.
Ammobium alatum grandiflorum (Everlasting Sand Flower)	Easy-to-grow annual. The flowers have silvery petals with yellow centres. Pick before flowers are fully open in July. Stems may need wiring.	As this is a true everlasting flower, pick and use straight away. Alternatively stand stems in a jar (with no water) until needed.

Classification	Plant material	Method of preservation
Anaphalis (Pearly Everlasting)	Easy-to-grow annual, which has silvery-grey foliage with clusters of tiny whitish flowers. Grows to 30–60 cm (1–2 ft) tall. Pick in summer when flowers appear.	Another true everlasting flower, but it benefits from a short spell of natural air-drying, hung in bunches.
Angelica	A hardy easy-to-grow biennial herb with clusters of yellowy-green flowers on long stalks. It grows 1·5–2·5 m (5–8 ft) high. Pick in mid- to late summer, whenever flowers are at their best and before they start to seed.	Dry naturally by hanging individually or in bunches.
Aquilegia vulgaris See page 20	Hardy herbaceous perennial. The long-spurred hybrids produce a good variety of colours with 60–90 cm (2–3 ft) high stems. Excellent for large arrangements. Pick in early to mid-summer.	Dry naturally by hanging individually or in bunches.
Artemisia abrotanum (Lad's Love, Southern Wood or Old Man)	Hardy semi-evergreen shrub, which is easy to grow and useful for either fresh or dried foliage. It grows 60–120 cm (2–4 ft) tall and has dull yellow flowers. Pick midsummer to early autumn.	Dry naturally by hanging in bunches.
Artichoke (Globe)	A perennial that is not always hardy. Generally grown as a vegetable, but the large flower heads which are 7·5–15 cm (3–6 in) across can be dried. They resemble a large Scotch thistle and the purple colouring fades to a lovely coffee to dark brown colour. Pick in early to mid-summer.	Dry naturally by hanging individual flower heads on stems.

Classification	Plant material	Method of preservation
Astilbe See page 23 	Hardy, easy-to-grow, herbaceous perennial, that, depending on variety, grows to a height of 60–180 cm (2–6 ft) and has feathery plumes of flowers. Pick in early to mid-summer.	Dry naturally by hanging in bunches.
Ballota 	A shrub belonging to the sage family. It is easy to grow, but should be cut back to ground level each autumn. This encourages the sprays (which dry well) to appear in the following spring. Pick them for drying in early to mid-summer.	Dry naturally by hanging in bunches.
Catananche caerulea (Cupid's Dart)	Hardy annual or short-lived perennial which needs a sunny position. Cornflower-like blue or white flowers on 45–75 cm (18–30 in) stems. Pick in mid- to late summer.	Dry naturally by hanging in bunches.
Delphinium ajacis (Larkspur) 	A hardy or half-hardy annual, that is related to the perennial delphiniums. Blue, purple, red, pink or white flower spikes appear from early to late summer and should be picked while the top flowers are still closed, for drying. Depending on the variety, the stems can reach a height of up to 120 cm (4 ft). Flowers have very pretty subtle colouring when dried.	Dry naturally by hanging in bunches.
Echinops (Globe Thistle)	A perennial, which, once established, is very prolific. The 90–120 cm (3–4 ft) tall stalks	Dry naturally by hanging individual flower heads by their stems.

Classification	Plant material	Method of preservation
Echinops (Globe Thistle) continued	are topped with spherical blue flowers that have a metallic sheen. These appear through mid- to late summer, but should be picked for drying before they are fully open. Like all members of the thistle family, they dry very well.	
Eryngium maritimum (Sea Holly)	Hardy perennial, that is easy to grow. Teasel-like, cone-shaped heads of metallic blue are surrounded by narrow blue bracts. It grows approximately 45 cm (18 in) tall and flowers from midsummer to autumn. Gather flowers for drying before they are fully mature; they dry most attractively.	Dry naturally by hanging in bunches.
Garrya elliptica	A tree or shrub that flowers in late winter with long, 'catkin-like', pale greeny-yellow flowers. Pick for drying as the flowers appear.	Dry naturally by hanging in bunches or preserve in glycerine.
Gomphrena globosa (Globe Amaranth)	Half-hardy annual, which is easy to grow given a sunny position. Grows approximately 30 cm (12 in) high, and has white, pink or purple globular flowers that appear from midsummer to autumn. Cut before flowers are fully open.	Dry naturally by hanging in bunches.
Helichrysum bracteatum (Strawflower)	An easy-to-grow annual which likes a good sunny position. It produces flowers that resemble a double daisy with stiff, shiny petals. They	This is a true everlasting flower. The stems do not dry well so if you want the flowers for an arrangement (as opposed to a picture), you

Classification	Plant material	Method of preservation
Helichrysum bracteatum (Strawflower) continued (Also *Helichrysum augustifolium*, see opposite, a perennial grown for its foliage)	come in a wide variety of colours, from white through to golden orange and deep russet red. There are dwarf and taller varieties, ranging from 45–120 cm (18 in–4 ft) tall. Pick before the petals can be easily pulled off, or the centre of the flower begins to come away.	will have to give them false stems (see page 41). Flower heads will dry anywhere – in boxes placed in the airing cupboard for example. If you want helichrysum for flower-balls (see page 60), it is essential to push small wires into the centre *before* the flower dries, so it will shrink and hold the wire in place securely.
Helipterum manglesii (Margles Sunray)	An annual which is easy to grow given a good sunny position. It grows 30–40 cm (12–18 in) tall, and has clusters of tiny daisy-like flowers in white, pink or rose.	A true everlasting flower that, therefore, needs minimal preservation treatment. Dry naturally by hanging in bunches.
Helipterum roseum (Rose Sunray)	An annual which also likes a sunny position. In a really good summer, it can flower six weeks after it has been sown. The 60 cm (2 ft) tall stalks support pink, daisy-like flowers. A white variety is also available, called *Helipterum album*.	As for *Helipterum manglesii*.
Moluccella laevis (Bells of Ireland or Shell Flower)	A half-hardy annual, which grows best in a light, rich soil and an open, sunny position. It grows approximately 60 cm (2 ft) tall and has spikes of fragrant white flowers, each surrounded with a bell-like, pale green calyx. This looks very striking in a dried arrangement. Pick when the top flowers are closed; usually in mid- to late summer.	Dry naturally by hanging in bunches.

Classification	Plant material	Method of preservation
Nicandra (Shoo-fly or Peruvian Apple) See picture opposite	A hardy annual that grows to a height of approximately 90 cm (3 ft). It flowers from midsummer to autumn, but do not pick for drying until the fruit (globular and enclosed by bright green and purple calyces) appears. This is generally from late summer to mid-autumn. Pick when branches have a collection of fruit on them.	Dry naturally by hanging in bunches.
Limonium vulgare-statice (Sea Lavender) 	An annual, often found growing wild around coasts and salt marshes. It grows 30 cm (1 ft) tall and has textured flowers of blue, mauve or white. A taller variety, *Limonium latifolium* has mauve flowers and grows to a height of 90 cm (3 ft). There is also a yellow annual, *Limonium bonduelli* (Algerian Sea Lavender) which grows from 30–60 cm (1–2 ft) tall. All these varieties dry well and are treated in a similar way. Pick in late summer.	Dry naturally by hanging in bunches.
Seed heads and berries Althaea (Hollyhock)	These grow best treated as biennials. The 120–180 cm (4–6 ft) tall spikes of flowers appear from midsummer to autumn. Cut for drying when the last flower has dropped and the seed pods are swelling.	Dry naturally by hanging individually from the stems.
Allium albopilosum	This easy-to-grow bulbous plant is a member of the	Dry naturally by hanging individual heads from stems.

Classification	Plant material	Method of preservation
Digitalis purpurea (Foxglove)	onion family. Traces of the typical onion smell generally disappear during drying. It grows approximately 45 cm (18 in) tall and flowers in early summer. It has huge umbels or seed heads, up to 15 cm (6 in) across, of lilac-pink, star-shaped flowers. Pick in midsummer. (Try drying chives and leeks as well when the flower heads have appeared).	
Allium albopilosum continued 	Generally biennial, this plant, which grows prolifically in the English countryside has 90 cm (3 ft) spikes of purple, red or maroon flowers. These appear in early summer; pick for drying when the last flowers have dropped and the seed pods are swelling. The cultivated garden varieties have a wider range of colours, and carry the flowers all round the spikes.	Dry naturally by hanging in bunches, or preserve by the glycerine method. Pick at the same time if preserving this way; they will look like honey-coloured orchids after two to three weeks in the glycerine solution.
Dipsacus sylvestris (The Common Teasel or Venus Cup) See picture opposite	These biennials are generally found by rivers and streams, but can also be grown easily from seed. According to variety, they will reach heights of 120–180 cm (4–6 ft). Pick in late summer, when seed pods are ripening. (Be careful – the stems are prickly!)	Seed pods will be dry when you pick them and are ready for use. Alternatively, store them until you want them, by hanging in bunches.
Lunaria (Honesty)	An easy-to-grow biennial which has white or purple flowers. These appear on stalks 45–90 cm (18 in– 3 ft) high. In summer, the	Dry naturally by hanging in bunches. If you pick seed pods when they are greeny-purple, you can preserve them by the glycerine method.

Classification	Plant material	Method of preservation
Lunaria (Honesty) continued 	flat oval seed pods change from green to silvery-white. Gather for dried arrangements when pods begin to change colour; if you leave them on the plant to dry, they become too brittle. Try experimenting with drying sprays by picking seed pods while they are still green.	
Papaver (Poppy Seed Heads) 	These are easy to grow either as annuals or perennials. They produce a variety of seed head sizes and stem lengths. Gather when petals have fallen and seed pods are swelling in early summer.	Dry naturally by hanging individually or in bunches.
Physalis franchetii (Cape Gooseberry) See picture opposite	A hardy perennial. Grown for the brilliant orange fruits, enclosed in a papery, orange-red calyx. Pick as this changes colour from green to orange, which is usually in early autumn, and it will keep its colour well during drying. If the lanterns get squashed during storage, you can sometimes restore the shape by making a pinhole at one end and blowing gently into it. Or slit them along the main ribs or stems and curl the orange covering back to form 'petals'.	The 'lanterns' dry easily and well. Hang them in small bunches or individually and leave them to dry naturally.
Rose hips, or other autumn berries, such as hawthorn, spindle, iris seed heads etc.	These will often keep their colour right through autumn and winter while still on the plant. Pick as the berries ripen and change colour from green to orange and red.	Either hang to dry, or, using a small artist's brush, give berries a coat of clear varnish.

Classification	Plant material	Method of preservation
Wild seed heads, such as dock, sorrel, hemlock, giant hogweed, campions, cow parsley, plantains and poppies	The flowering periods of these run from late spring onwards, through the summer. In general, gather all varieties about the time the seed heads are changing colour. This is not always possible, so be prepared to experiment with small quantities as you are able to pick them. You will often have very successful results with unusual colouring if you pick them a little early, although they may not keep as long.	Dry all naturally by hanging individually or in bunches. (Many will be almost dry when you pick them.)
Grasses: wild and cultivated	There is a wide selection of ornamental grasses, some of which are listed below. These can easily be grown from seed, but restrict them to one area, or to a window box. There are also endless varieties of decorative grasses growing wild, but do remember when picking in the countryside, to restrict yourself to a few of each variety. *All* grasses should be picked quite early in summer before they are fully mature, so they do not shed their seeds.	Dry naturally by hanging in bunches. Try drying some by placing upright in a jar, to produce 'droopier' stems.
Agrostis nebulosa (Cloud Grass)	Sown in autumn, this variety grows to 45 cm (18 in) tall and produces a 'cloudy' head which looks as if it consists of a mass of tiny flowers.	As above.
Briza maxima (Pearl Grass)	An annual, it has stalks 45 cm (18 in) high of small hanging 'pendants'. These move gently in any breeze.	As above.

Classification	Plant material	Method of preservation
Coix lacryma-jobi (Job's Tears)	Annual grass which produces 60–90 cm (2–3 ft) tall stems with thick, maize-like leaves and, later, grey-green seeds.	As above.
Cortaderia (Pampas Grass) 	Perennial evergreen grasses, from 1·2–3 m (4–10 ft) in height according to variety. In general, they have slender arching leaves, with rough edges, so take great care when cutting. The stems carry silky plumes that may be white, silvery-white or silver-purple. For best results, pick as plumes are just emerging from their sheath.	As above.
Eragrostis elegans (Love Grass)	A feathery graceful annual of a deep green colour that grows to a height of 60–90 cm (2–3 ft).	As above.
Lagurus ovatus (Hare's Tail) See picture opposite	An annual which grows 30–45 cm (12–18 in) high, with silky, creamy-coloured heads.	As above.
Triticum Spelta (Ornamental wheat)	All these can be grown for ornamental purposes and will dry well.	As above.
Wheat, barley (see page 32), oats, sweet corn or maize and millet	This can be grown as an annual and is a very decorative wheat grass.	As above, but also try picking some green and drying them in silica gel or borax.
Foliage	The following are just a few of the foliage varieties that may be preserved satisfactorily. As with any other	Nearly all sprays of foliage may be successfully preserved using the glycerine method.

material, pick sprays in good condition, when they are dry, with undamaged leaves. The colours of the leaves will vary considerably depending on the time of year you pick them as well as on the variety. Preserved colour can range from a creamy-white, through tan, chestnut brown or greeny-bronze. Pick the leaves when they are mature, but not when they are so old that the sap has stopped rising. In such a case, the stem will not be able to take up the glycerine solution. In fact, you can pick most species of foliage from late spring through to early autumn, and you will get varying results of colour from the sprays you preserve at different times. Towards mid-autumn, most foliage begins to get woody, at which time it is really no good for preserving. Do remember, incidentally, to use your discretion when picking branches and stems, both from trees in your own garden and from those in the countryside. Particularly when picking towards the end of the season, you are discouraging next year's growth, and it is all too easy to 'strip' a tree at this point, so that it is a very sorry spectacle indeed the following spring.

| Camellia | Beautiful deep-green glossy foliage. Pick after flowering in late spring. | Glycerine method. |

Classification	Plant material	Method of preservation
Choisya ternala (Mexican Orange Blossom) See picture opposite	Cut sprays from spring to midsummer. The leaves will change to a lovely warm, creamy colour, as they absorb the glycerine.	Glycerine method.
Elaeagnus 	Hardy evergreen or deciduous shrubs, grown for their attractive foliage. Colours vary from silvery-grey to creamy-yellow and gold splashed leaves. Cut sprays for preserving in late spring and early summer.	Glycerine method.
Eucalyptus 	Native to Australia and Tasmania, the variety most commonly grown in the UK is *E. gunnii*. According to the age of the tree, the leaf colour will vary from silvery-white, through blue-green to a deep, dark green. Cut from spring onwards.	Glycerine method
Fagus sylvatica (Beech)	Probably the easiest foliage to preserve, cut from early summer to early autumn, to get a variety of shades.	Glycerine method. Check regularly. If left too long, the leaves can become heavy and oily.
Laurel Common (see page 36) or Portuguese	Pick in spring before flowering occurs.	Glycerine method.
Oak, elm, lime flowers, sweet chestnut and hornbeam seeds	Pick sprays from spring onwards, making sure you choose only those in good condition. Strip the leaves from the branches of lime, leaving only the flowers on the spray.	Glycerine method. If the ends of the stems are too hard, split or crush them and dip them in boiling water for a few seconds, before placing in glycerine mixture.

Classification	Plant material	Method of preservation
Senecio maritimus and *Senecio laxifolius*  	Both these varieties are useful as they keep their silvery-grey leaf colouring when dried or preserved. Pick sprays in the spring and again when flower buds develop, but *before* they open.	Dry naturally by hanging in bunches, or preserve by the glycerine method.
Wild Clematis (Old Man's Beard)	Cut when the foliage has turned green in late spring, and then again in late summer when the leaves are changing colour from green to beigy-cream. This will give different effects.	Glycerine method, but leave sprays in the solution for two to three days only, then hang up in bunches to dry.

In addition to the flowers, shrubs, grasses etc. mentioned in the guide, collect all varieties of larch, pine and fir cones. They are invaluable in all manner of decorations. Keep them separate from the more delicate dried or preserved material.

Many of the varieties included in the classification may be bought at florists' shops, together with dyed, dried plant material. These are costly to buy, so check the stems and heads before buying to make sure you are really getting the best. Look for some more unusual flowers, such as protea or the South African lily. Although quite expensive to buy, they will last for years if properly stored. (See *Storage*, page 17.)

Skeletonizing leaves

A skeletonized leaf is one where all the soft green matter has been removed, leaving a delicate structure of veins. This skeletonization occurs naturally when leaves fall to the ground and the soft part is eaten by insects, or rots away. Search under trees and shrubs and you might find some, although they will often be damaged. Skeletonized leaves are very pretty in delicate arrangements or for use in pictures. Leaves can also be skeletonized on the stem.

To skeletonize leaves at home, select a handful of leaves in good condition. The tough types are best — laurel, camellia, magnolia, ivy, holly and ficus are all suitable. Add a handful of washing soda to a pan of warm water, stir until it is dissolved and drop in the leaves. Simmer very gently for one to two hours. Then test a leaf; if the green covering is soft enough, it will rub or scrape off with a knife under cold running water. Do this *very* carefully, otherwise you might damage the veins. Rinse the leaves when you have removed all the green part and dry between sheets of soft kitchen paper or blotting paper.

Usually the leaves are a dull brown at this stage, but they can be lightened if you prefer by soaking them in a mixture of domestic bleach and water (1 tablespoon bleach to 600 ml [1 pint] water) for 12 hours. Rinse and dry carefully and store as for other preserved material, flat in boxes.

Below: Leaves with a pronounced network of veins are attractive when skeletonized.

Preparation of material

You can ensure the greatest possible use of much of your dried material if you spend a little time and trouble on it first. Wiring flowers or leaves not only serves to lengthen the stems, but also provides a more supple or malleable support, thereby giving greater flexibility in use. Florists' wires are the most suitable for this operation and they can generally be purchased in bundles of 20 from most good florists or garden centres; 22 gauge is the most suitable for the more delicate flowers, and 18 gauge for the heavier material. If you need extra strength to support a particularly heavy flower head, twist two of the finer wires together.

Remember that it is *essential* to wire everlasting flowers and those dried in silica gel *before* the flowers are dried. This applies particularly to the true everlastings (such as helichrysum and helipterum), as they tend to have a very short, brittle stem after drying. Cut with about 2·5 cm (1 in) of stem; then, if the stem of the flower is soft or hollow, push the wire through the stem and into the base of the flower, taking care not to penetrate the front of the bloom.

If the flower has a tough or woody stem, however, just push the wire into the base beside the natural stem, twisting it round this to secure it.

You can always lengthen a short piece of wire later if you want to, by simply putting another piece of wire alongside the first, overlapping the two by about 2·5 cm (1 in) and binding the two wires together with fine fuse or copper wire.

To neaten false stems, and give them a more 'natural' appearance, bind round them with gutta percha tape which is available from most florists and garden centres. This is a plastic self-adhesive tape in various shades of green and brown. When binding, hold the flower in your right hand and start binding at the top of the stem just underneath the head. Twist the tape round the stem, guiding it between your fingers and pressing it together firmly when you get to the bottom of the stem. It is an easy operation to carry out, but one that greatly enhances the appearance of the flower.

Dried hollow corn stalks can also be used to improve the appearance of false stems. Just slip them over the wires and fix in place with a minute dab of glue at the base of the flower. Alternatively tie at the base to prevent the corn stalk slipping down. A length of raffia can also be used for binding over the wire, but this will need sticking carefully at the top and bottom with a dab of glue.

Top: Helipterum is one of the true everlasting flowers (see page 25).

Bottom: Try making your own 'everlasting' flowers with assorted dried material.

41

Wiring leaves

Small or limp leaves often need supporting to keep them rigid, or they may require a longer stem. To provide this, place a single piece of wire along the centre back, and hold it in position with a length of clear sticky tape.

To support larger leaves, make a loop of wire, lay it on the back of the leaf, and secure it in the same way.

Bunches or clusters of flowers

These are useful as a focal or central point when making a large arrangement, or combined with grasses and leaves to make a Victorian posy. Select flowers according to colour and size; most clusters are made from the smaller everlastings, but there are no hard and fast rules and it can always be an area of experiment.

A cluster: Wire flowers before drying. Prepare some by inserting a loop of wire through the front of the flowers and pulling this through just far enough to ensure the wire is hidden. Twist the two ends of the wire together under the head. Use a flower wired in this way as the centre point, adding others around it as required. Bind all stems together with thin copper wire, finishing off with gutta percha tape if necessary.

A posy: Begin with a centre flower, wired with a long stalk, as described for a cluster. Add leaves and flowers at different levels and angles symmetrically around it, twisting wires together as you go. Bend the material outwards away from the centre, as you work, until you have a posy that is the size and shape you require. As a final pretty touch, finish off the posy by pushing the stalks through the centre of a doily and gathering it up around the flowers.

Branch or spike of flowers

A branch or spike of flowers is useful for providing height in an arrangement. Grade the flowers in sizes putting the smallest at the top, as they would grow naturally. The topmost flower therefore needs to have a long stem, while the rest of the flowers or leaves should have stems approximately 7·5–10 cm (3–4 in) long. Use gutta percha plastic tape to hold the flowers in place. Begin by binding the long stem for 2·5 cm (1 in), then place the head of the second flower just under the head of the first and bind the stems together. Continue adding flowers and/or leaves until the spike or branch reaches the length you want it to be. When completed, bend flowers and leaves into natural-looking positions.

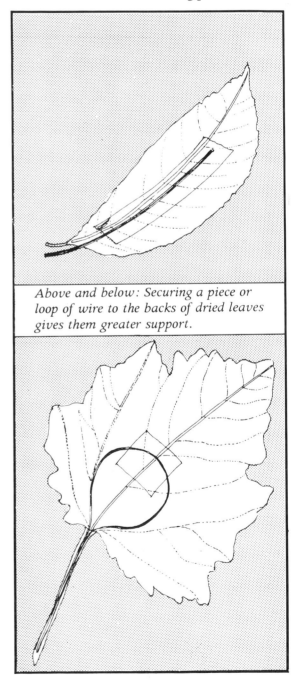

Above and below: Securing a piece or loop of wire to the backs of dried leaves gives them greater support.

Posy

The extremely pretty posy below is made of statice and helichrysum flowers framed by a border of beech leaves. It is made exactly as described in the instructions, with all the material wired on to the central flower. Careful positioning of colours is the key to success in such a posy, and note how the deeper colours are cleverly positioned for evenness of effect. The statice in this instance relieves the otherwise slight 'flatness' of the flowers, some of which have been very slightly recessed rather than all positioned at the same height. Note, too, that they are not all placed at the same angle. The other important factor to bear in mind when planning a posy is that the material you use must be absolutely perfect. The beech leaves, for example, are all much the same size and perfectly shaped. Never use tatty or blemished material in a posy; it will show up like a sore thumb!

Below: A circle of beech leaves provides the perfect frame for this posy.

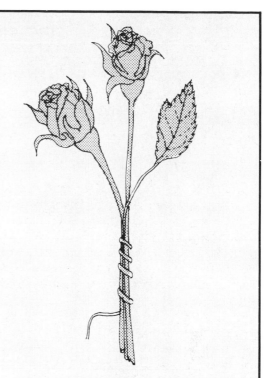

Above: Begin with the central flower of a posy and wire others to it.

Below: Build the design downwards and outwards from the central point.

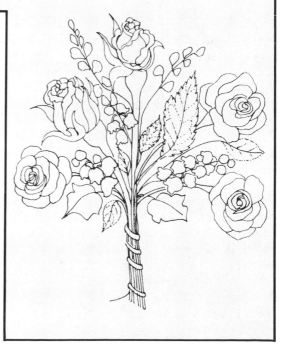

Dyeing grasses

Dyed grasses and flowers can be bought at many florists and will provide bright splashes of colour where required. However, they are relatively expensive and the process of dyeing can be easily carried out at home. Not only, of course, is this considerably cheaper, but it often provides a wider range of more delicate colourings.

Dyeing with food colourings: Make a basic mixture in a jam jar of 1 tablespoon of colouring to 125 ml (4 fl oz) of cold water and mix well. If you are dyeing dried grasses, immerse the heads in the container of dye and leave them for several hours. When they are the colour you want, dry off on sheets of newspaper and hang in small bunches in an airy, dry, dark place.

You can also dye fresh grasses, and although this tends to be less reliable, it is worth trying. Mix the dye in the same way, then immerse the grasses, stalks first, in the container and leave them for up to 12 hours to absorb the dye through their stems. Hang in small bunches in an airy, dry, dark place.

If, after dyeing, some of your grasses are too brilliant a colour, simply place in the sun for a few hours. Turn them occasionally, and leave them until the sunlight has faded them to the colour you want.

Some flowers, such as 'Esther Read' daisies can also be dyed at home, and then dried. When experimenting with dyeing flowers, white flowers produce the most consistently reliable results. In particular, beautiful shades of green can be achieved, according to strength of dye and conditions when drying. Follow the same procedure here as for dyeing grasses.

Multi-purpose, cold-water dyes, as sold for fabrics, can also be used for dyeing plant material. In this case make up the dye as instructed on the label. Remember to use an old saucepan or container, and try a small quantity first, to determine the amount of dye you need to use for each bunch of grasses or flowers. Hold the material you are going to dye by the stalks, and immerse the heads in

the solution, turning the material once or twice so it soaks up the dye evenly. When you have done this leave them for a few hours, checking occasionally, until they appear to be the colour you want. Have some

sheets of old newspaper ready and lay the plant material out on this to dry, then hang it upside down for a short period of air-drying. Incidentally, never use hot-water dyes for dyeing plant material.

Some wood stains, brushed lightly on to selected plant material, can often give pleasing colours. This is an economical method, but take care when doing it, as you only need a very little of the stain. Use a small brush – if you put too much stain on the plant it just becomes sodden.

Below: Grasses of all kinds are the perfect material to dye at home, and look delightful standing against a pine background (inset).

Arrangements using cones

Pine or fir cones look very effective in arrangements if some of the cones are bleached, so that you have a two-tone effect. Soak the cones for a short period in strong household bleach; wear rubber gloves and either work out of doors or in a well-ventilated room, as the fumes from bleach can be strong. Leave the cones in the bleach for a few minutes until they reach the required colour, then remove and shake them carefully (making sure you do not splash yourself or your clothes) to remove as much moisture as possible. Lay them on paper in front of a fan heater to dry; in this case, if you leave them to dry naturally, the cones may close up as they dry.

Small or medium-sized cones can make an excellent focal point in an arrangement, if combined with the seed pods of honesty to make a natural-looking 'flower'.

Take a length of florists' wire, double it over, and slide the top of the loop into the lower half of the cone (see diagrams). Push the wire in firmly, then bring the two ends of wire together underneath the cone, and twist them into a single stem. Put a small spot of clear glue or adhesive on the edge of an honesty seed pod, and insert this between opened 'petals' of the cone. Continue doing this, working from the base of the cone upwards and being careful not to overcrowd it. As a rough guide, about 24 'pods' will be sufficient for a small to medium-sized cone. Dried or pressed leaves, such as beech, can also be combined with cones in the same way, or you can make fir-cone 'flowers' using single eucalyptus or beech leaves.

When working with dried material, use the smallest quantity of adhesive or glue you possibly can. A pair of tweezers can be a help in holding small or fragile pieces as you glue them in place. If the adhesive is in a small bottle or jar, rather than a tube, a metal skewer is very useful for transferring small spots of glue from one piece of material to another. It also helps to prevent unwanted blobs of adhesive getting all over the place.

Above: Wired fir cones are invaluable for all manner of dried arrangements.

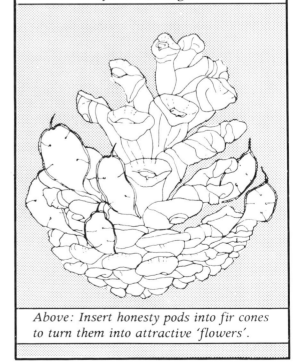

Above: Insert honesty pods into fir cones to turn them into attractive 'flowers'.

If you wish you can make other 'flowers' by combining the outside sheath or covering from the cobs of sweet corn with small cones or poppy seed heads.

Wire the cone, as already described. Then slip a hollow corn stalk over the wire and fix it to the base of the cone with a spot of glue. Now take a piece of the corn sheath and double it over. Place this under the base of the cone and tie it tightly to the stalk with fuse wire. Repeat this four times, with separate pieces of corn sheath, binding tightly each time. Then take a length of green or brown gutta percha tape, and starting at the top (beneath the cone), cover the wiring, whilst binding the corn 'petals' to the wire stalk. Continue down the stalk, fixing the tape with a dab of glue, if necessary, at the bottom of the stalk. These corn 'petals' are very strong, and can easily be coaxed into very natural-looking positions.

Follow exactly the same procedure if you are using a poppy seed head as the centre of the flower, but use smaller pieces of the corn sheath as 'petals' or they will swamp the seed head. Always make the 'petals' of a size proportionate to the centre point, whatever it might be. An odd number of petals gives a more natural appearance to the 'flower'.

Below: Slip stems over the twisted wires.

The stiff, dried stalks of Michaelmas daisies are very useful in making 'flowers', as they can be used over and over again to form a base. Just stick a small cone or seed head to the top of the stalk with a dab of adhesive and then layer leaves, flower petals or small pieces of dried fern or bracken around it. Dried seed pods of lupins, split in half, make superb 'petals' for use in this way.

Large pine cone 'flowers' make attractive 'mobiles'. Attach a loop of ribbon for hanging to the top and stick or wire on leaves, heads of flowers, or a combination as you like.

Small gourds and nuts or the 'saucers' from acorns can also be very useful in arrangements. Cover gourds with a coat of clear varnish and drill two small holes near the base to push wires through, if you want them for an arrangement. You could drill holes in nuts and wire them in clusters for arrangements too.

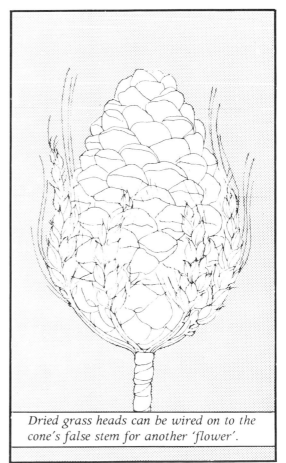

Dried grass heads can be wired on to the cone's false stem for another 'flower'.

Dried flower arrangements

In arranging dried and preserved plant material, very much the same principles as those that apply to fresh flowers should be followed. Dried arrangements have a number of obvious advantages; they do not twist or move out of shape after being arranged and are infinitely more adaptable; as they do not require water, a far greater variety of containers can be used; they can be placed in more inaccessible places, where factors such as a source of heat or shortage of light make the position unsuitable for fresh arrangements and, of course, they last considerably longer than fresh flower arrangements.

As with fresh flowers, dried plant material needs to be supported in the container if you are to be able to make the most of it. The supports most commonly used are florist's foam or styrofoam, wire mesh, Plasticine, pin holders or a detergent mix (see below). When asking for foam in a florist's shop, do say it is wanted for a dried arrangement as different types are sold for fresh and dried flowers. Foam is probably the easiest thing to use, but it is very light and overbalances easily. It must, therefore, be anchored firmly to the container, either by impaling it on a pin holder which is heavy enough itself to stay in place, or an 'oasis holder' which will have to be kept in place in the container with oasis fix, Plasticine or Blu-tack. Alternatively you can cover the foam with wire mesh and then tie the mesh to the container with thin ordinary wire. Styrofoam, which can be bought from most craft shops, is very useful for flower arrangements. Similar in texture to polystyrene, it does not crumble. It is available in all shapes and sizes – domes, balls, cones, logs, pyramids and so on. If you have difficulty in pushing woody stalks into it, make a hole first in the foam with a piece of wire and then push the stalk into place.

Wire mesh does not always give a close enough surface to hold the fine stems of some dried material. Detergent mix, which is made by mixing two tablespoons of water with one breakfast cup of detergent, takes about one hour to set before it is ready for use. It can be used again and again.

Whatever support you use, do make sure it is firm and secure in the container before you begin your arrangement. If the container is too light for the material, weight it with flower clay or Plasticine, or, if it is a deep type of container, you could put a handful or two of gravel in the bottom for weight.

If you want to do an arrangement which has fresh material as well as dried, use one of the special tubes designed for this purpose. These come in all sizes and are available at florists' shops. They should be filled either with water or soft foam and the fresh flowers

inserted into them. An acceptable 'do-it-yourself' substitute would be a small glass or plastic tube or bottle, such as those in which cake decorations are sold. Whatever type of tube or glass you use, tape it to the container or to a strong stem within the arrangement, and spray or paint it a neutral colour which will blend with the arrangement.

Containers for arrangements

Almost any containers can be used for dried arrangements, although clear glass would not be suitable if you could see through it to a mess of foam or wired stems. (The stalks of some dried material, however, – such as oats, barley and wheat – can be quite decorative.) Look out for small wicker, hedgerow or rush baskets, stone or earthenware jugs, jars and teapots, slabs of wood, shells, cooking and kitchen utensils such as bread tins, copper or china jelly moulds, candlesticks and rush table mats. These are just a few suggestions – with a little imagination, you could make use of almost anything!

Right and below: Almost anything can be used as a container for dried arrangements.

Formal arrangements

These arrangements need a basic outline, a focal point and material suitable for 'infilling'. Collect your dried material with these factors in mind, and remember that different textures and shapes, as well as colours, help to make more interesting arrangements.

Select three tall, rigid-stemmed pieces of material to give you the outer extremities of height and width. As a general rule these should be between one and a half to three times the length of a shallow container or height of a tall container. Put them in place first, with the three stems issuing from a central point.

After positioning them, select three slightly shorter-stemmed pieces of material. These should be fairly impressive. Put them in place, then, working towards the centre of the container, position a few even shorter-stemmed pieces of material, which are important in forming the main outline of the arrangement.

Now you must establish and position the arrangement's focal point, which should be something imposing such as a large hydrangea head, a cluster of berries, a large cone 'flower', corn sheath 'flower' or dried globe artichoke, for example. For arrangements that are viewed from one side only, the focal point should come near the middle and low down towards the base of the arrangement. (Arrangements that will be viewed from all angles and are therefore more 'circular' in shape do not have a focal point as such.)

Once the outline and focal point of the arrangement have been established, you can begin to fill out the design with grasses, sprays of corn, iris leaves or what you will. Choose the material carefully so that it complements the focal point and does not detract from it in any way. Keep the paler colours of material to the outer edge and work in towards the focal point, using deeper shades as you get closer to the centre. Just how you position the 'filling material' depends entirely on the arrangement, but do not be tempted to fill in all the 'holes' or

Above: A beautifully-blended arrangement in soft, autumnal colours.

'spaces' that occur naturally in any arrangement. No arrangement should be packed tight. There is an old saying that applies to dried flower arrangements as much as it does to fresh; 'When in doubt; leave it out'!

Blend the sizes of the material within the arrangement, upgrading gradually from small to large, rather than changing from one thing to another with a sudden leap. Recess some of the material to give an impression of depth.

It is sensible to put all arrangements in the place which you intend to be their permanent position before you complete them. A formal arrangement, which is to be viewed from one side only, is suitable for landings, fireplaces, corner areas, mantelpieces – anywhere where it stands against a wall or solid background – and it can be varied in size.

Arrangements that are viewed from all sides are often 'formal' in design too, and are based on the same triangular formation as those to be viewed from one side only. Position the outline material first, and then work around the arrangement, filling in the design systematically. Remember to recess some larger flowers a little to give depth to the arrangement.

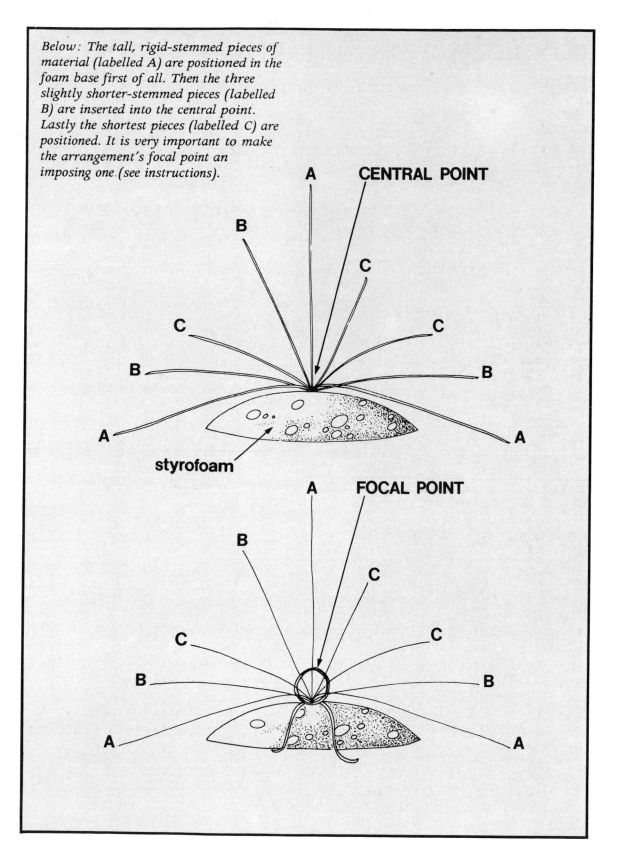

Below: The tall, rigid-stemmed pieces of material (labelled A) are positioned in the foam base first of all. Then the three slightly shorter-stemmed pieces (labelled B) are inserted into the central point. Lastly the shortest pieces (labelled C) are positioned. It is very important to make the arrangement's focal point an imposing one.(see instructions).

A

CENTRAL POINT

B

C

C

C

B

B

A

A

styrofoam

A

FOCAL POINT

B

C

C

C

B

B

A

A

Small formal 'bedroom' arrangement
This sweet little arrangement would be ideal for the bedside or dressing table in a guest's room. It is composed of very delicate material – helichrysum flowers, statice, mouse's ears, hare grass, hydrangea petals and pink pokers. It is the hare grass that gives this arrangement its softness. Note how the little china container perfectly complements the colours of the material used.

The tallest, central pink poker was put in position first, after which two circles of spikes were established. One of these is at the base of the arrangement, the other comes a little higher. The design was then filled in, working in a circle all the time to keep it symmetrical.

Circle or wreath

This arrangement could be used as a table centrepiece, perhaps with a toning candle in an attractive holder put in the middle, or it could be hung on a door or wall. It can be worked on a ring of foam, but in fact this one started life as a wire coat hanger! This was bent into a circle and then bound with gutta

percha tape.

The material used here includes beech leaves, cones, cotoneaster and helichrysum flowers. All the material is wired, both to provide a means of securing it to the circle and also to give it rigidity. (This applies particularly to the beech leaves which would otherwise be rather limp.)

The basic outline of beech leaves was worked first, the wires being twisted on to the coat hanger circle. Then the cones and flowers were twisted on together. Note how the size of the cones is absolutely correct for the other material used. The size ratio of material is very important in an arrangement of this nature – do make sure that nothing is swamped by something next to it which is just far too big. Note, too, how the flowers in particular are positioned at angles, some pointing in towards the centre and some pointing slightly outwards. Again, this is very important; if they were all positioned to point straight upwards, the design would be very flat and uninteresting.

When you have finished wiring on the material stand back and look at it again – you may find you need to add another leaf or two here and there.

Left: Fir cones merge perfectly with the rich colours of the wreath.

Below: Having bound the wire circle that forms the base of the wreath, wire the material to it, keeping it tightly packed together to avoid obvious 'holes'. Make as perfect a circle as possible.

Asymmetrical triangle arrangements

Arrangements following the main outline of an asymmetrical triangle look very effective in 'pedestal'-type containers. Select two tall, rigid-stemmed pieces of material to act as 'A' in the diagram. One of these will be the perpendicular line of the triangle and is positioned to establish the topmost point of the arrangement. The other piece should be positioned at right angles to it, coming from the same spot. Select two shorter-stemmed pieces of material to act as the 'A2's and position them. Again, they should emanate from the same point as the two already positioned. You now have the main outline of the arrangement and can fill in with the remainder of the material. Keep the deeper colours to the centre and low down, over the point where the main stems converge.

Asymmetrical triangle arrangement in basket

Although there is definitely a 'front view' to this arrangement, it has been carefully worked so that it looks neat and attractive from all angles. It would make an ideal arrangement for a corner table in a room. The material used included the following: beech leaves, holly leaves, helichrysum flowers, poppy seeds, statice, hydrangea petals and pink pokers. It was worked in an old-fashioned rose basket with a piece of foam wired to the bottom. The important point to remember when working an arrangement in this sort of container is to make only one side of the arrangement higher than the handle. Bearing that in mind, the design is worked in the usual way, beginning by positioning the tallest material and following this with those that establish the width. You will see it has a 'loose' line with 'flow' and movement. The spiky shapes of the material bend in a variety of directions and help to achieve this. Also, less material is used, so the effect is generally more airy and less concentrated. Once the height, width and flow of the design are established, it is filled in with the other material, recessing some to give depth and interest.

Top: This arrangement was worked by wiring a piece of oasis to the middle of the basket. Similarly shaped arrangements could be made in tall containers.

Below: Establish the outline of the arrangement before filling in the centre.

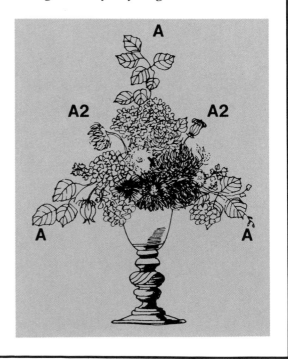

Informal arrangement

This can consist of more or less any material you have available at the time you want to make it, and it will often have other bits and pieces added to it or substituted for those already in it. The 'informality' refers to the lack of rigidity or symmetry in design and also in the use of container, which can be as unconventional as you like! Some interesting suggestions would be a stone jam jar, a jug, teapot, pewter or china tankard.

It is obviously hard to give rigid principles to follow as, by definition, such arrangements are totally personal and individual. However, try to make sure you include one or two splashes of colour – such as rich helichrysum flowers on wires. Also, the heads of dried sweet corn provide a definite shape that is a good foil for seed heads, grasses or the feathery plumes of pampas or astilbe.

If your arrangement is to stand in a warm, light room, you could include fresh stalks of green material, which will then dry in the arrangement. Or add a few fresh flowers to the design, replacing them with others, or with dried material as they die.

Informal arrangement in pewter mug
The colours and shape of this charming arrangement were dictated by the pewter mug which was chosen as a container. Note how the line of the design has been taken *away* from the handle; this is achieved by the sloping line of deeply coloured helichrysum which leads your eye down the design in a curve. This takes the place of the focal point of a more formal arrangement; when it is the container that is the important feature of an arrangement, the design does not need a focal point. It is essential in such an instance not to smother the line of the container.

The plant material used in this design features beech leaves, laurel leaves, poppy seed heads, old man's beard, helichrysum flowers and ballota.

Festive and special arrangements

For Christmas and other festive occasions, try combining dried and fresh materials, and incorporating fruit, gourds or glass baubles into the design. Look out for the artificial Christmas roses which are now available and are most effective. Mix them with holly, ivy, silvered or gilded seed heads and dried material to make a very colourful centrepiece for the table. For such an arrangement use a fairly low, oblong container, such as a bread tin, and fill it with crumpled wire mesh. If you want to include candles in the arrangement, wedge these firmly in position first, then put sprigs of holly or ivy round the base of the candles. Fill in around these, building outwards to the edges of the design.

If you are using glass baubles as well, particularly medium to large ones, keep them towards the centre of the arrangement. Mass the material so that it covers the 'mechanics' of the arrangement (i.e. the foam or whatever you are using to hold the material) and flows down towards the table top. Apart from using candles, never build a table centrepiece so high that it impedes conversation because people cannot see one another over the top of it.

If you want to spray material, perhaps silver or gold, for a Christmas or anniversary arrangement, do remember it is very invasive and a little can go an awful long way! Cover the whole of your working area with newspaper, and hold the aerosol can approximately 12·5–15 cm (5–6 in) away from the material you are spraying. You can make a pretty silver wedding arrangement by using silvery-grey or grey-green dried materials, adding silvered cones, seed heads and white and silvered fronds of fern. Equally for a golden wedding anniversary arrangement, use sprigs of gold and green variegated holly, yellow and gold helichrysum, dried yarrow and gilded seed heads and grasses.

Right: Coloured balls and decorative ribbons are a great help in the making of a 'special occasion' arrangement.

Christmas decoration
This design worked in a low (hidden) plastic container is based on a formal design and was arranged accordingly. Because the container is a lightweight one and the material is obviously quite heavy, the container has been weighted with a heavy pin holder and then packed with foam.

The festive arrangement has been worked with a mixture of preserved plant material and artificial sprays as well as the Christmas baubles and a big bow of silver ribbon. These latter items obviously provide the focal point, and you will see that they are positioned low down in the arrangement.

The plant material used included cones (some of which were sprayed with a gilt spray), poppy seed heads (also gilded), sprigs of holly and verbascum (both sprayed bronze), chestnut and laurel leaves and the beautiful, exotic sea holly flowers which have been sprayed too. The silver fern you can see is artificial.

Incidentally, when you are spraying material to get a golden effect for an arrangement, a dull bronze or gilt gives an infinitely more attractive finish than a brighter gold paint.

Below: A gay Christmas arrangement.

Table centrepiece (**three** candles)
This elegant table centrepiece has been
created from the following material:
beech leaves, hornbeam leaves, phlomis
(Jerusalem sage), nigella (love-in-a-mist),
four open and four closed cones, honesty
pods, poppy seed heads, liatris and
privet. It was arranged in a low copper
container packed with dried foam. It
would be equally suitable as a table
centrepiece or to stand on a chest or
sideboard if the candles had been
omitted. Notice how very slim candles
have been used so as to give the minimum of interference between people
across the table.

The circular outline of leaves was
established first and then the candles
were positioned. The cones which provide texture were put in next. They
have been positioned evenly around
the arrangement, but at slightly differ-
ing angles, to create an effect of balance
rather than perfect symmetry. After the
cones, the area around the candles was
filled in to make sure they were completely covered. Fairly lightweight material was used here, and the more solid
and dramatic material reserved for the
outer limits of the arrangement.
The 'infill' material was then put in to
complete the design; this was worked
around the arrangement in a 'circular'
movement. Note how some items have
been recessed to give depth. In this
kind of arrangement, i.e. one which is
low and will basically be viewed from
above, occasional gaps are necessary to
relieve the design.

*Right: In an arrangement of this type,
position the candles first, spacing them
evenly. Follow with the most dominant
items, making sure you work evenly all
round the arrangement. Fill in the design
but keep the highest point well away from
the top of the candles to avoid any fire
risk.*

Flower balls

These are cheap, simple and easy to make, yet can look very effective.

The essential items you need are a styrofoam ball, a knitting needle or skewer, florist's wire, wired flowers and ribbon. Begin by making a hole through the centre of the ball with the knitting needle. Fold a length of ribbon in half (the length depends on whether the finished ball is to be carried or hung). Bend a length of wire in half and then thread the wire through the loop of ribbon. Push the ends of the wire through the hole made with the knitting needle, and pull the ribbon through until about 2·5 cm (1 in) shows at the top. Now cover the ball with flowers, by pushing the wired stems into it, so that no foam is visible.

Any dried flowers can be used – helichrysum is particularly attractive – but the stems must be wired. According to the size of the ball, these stems should be about 2·5–5 cm (1–2 in) long. When you have almost covered the ball with flowers, press a knitting needle well into the foam and use it as a handle whilst completing the ball.

If you wish, you can add small ribbon bows to the ball. Cut a length of wire 2·5 cm (1 in) long, bend in half and slip a piece of ribbon through it. Tie this into a bow, then push it into the foam between the flowers. Choose the ribbon to tone or contrast with the flowers, whichever you feel will look most effective.

A double flower ball, made with a small and large ball of styrofoam, is also most attractive. It is made by threading the ribbon through the small ball first, leaving a 2·5 cm (1 in) length of ribbon to be threaded through the larger ball. These would make a lovely change from a more conventional bouquet for bridesmaids.

Flower ball
This was made exactly following the directions given above. It is the choice of colours that is of prime importance – here we have used shades of pink flowers and teamed them up with delicate green and pink ribbon. The whole effect is one of spring freshness. Compare this with the more mellow, autumnal look of the posy.

As the wires in the flowers have to be very firm to stick into the foam in a flower ball, it is really essential that they are inserted through the centre of the flowers as soon as the flowers are picked – i.e. before drying takes place. Thus, as the flowers dry and shrink naturally, they will hold firmly on to the wire.

The ribbon was curled by running the flat side of a knife firmly along it.

Right: This delicately coloured flower ball would make a lovely change from a traditional bouquet for a bridesmaid to carry at a spring or summer wedding.

Flower tree or cone

You can buy styrofoam cones for these arrangements, or you can make your own from wire mesh. Remember that it is *essential* that the cone, whether foam or mesh, should be attached firmly to the chosen container. This is generally one that will give height to the tree, such as a cake stand or something similar. To make a wire mesh cone, you will need:

☐ Brown paper, newspaper or similar for a pattern
☐ Wire mesh with 1 cm ($\frac{1}{2}$ in) holes
☐ Wire cutters or good strong scissors
☐ Fine wire or string
☐ Adhesive tape
☐ Crumbled florist's foam

Cut a square of paper and fold it in half to make a triangle. Join the two short sides with adhesive tape to make a cone shape, then cut the base evenly so that the cone stands upright. Cut the tape and place this pattern flat on a piece of wire mesh. Cut around the pattern with wire cutters or shears, then join the edges to make a cone, by binding together with fine wire or string. Line the inside of the cone with the paper pattern, and fill with crumbled foam, packing it in as tightly as you can. Seal the base of the cone by cutting a circle of paper or cardboard to cover the foam. Put this in place and secure with several strips of adhesive tape placed across it at right angles.

A 30 cm (12 in) square of paper will produce a finished cone 30 cm (12 in) high with a circumference of approximately 45 cm (18 in) round the base.

All the dried material etc. that you intend to use to make the 'tree' should be wired first. Gather everything together and decide how you are going to use it. Start at the base of the cone with the largest and heaviest items. Grade the material as you progress upwards, so that the smallest and lightest comes at the top.

A very simple, but very effective 'tree', can be made by combining natural and bleached fir cones and beech nut shells. For a Christmas 'tree', sprigs of holly, gilded or silvered seed heads, small glass baubles and scarlet and green ribbon provide an arrangement that will last through the twelve days of Christmas and beyond!

If you are using a foam cone, try making a spiral arrangement with dried flowers, either using contrasting colours or varying shades of one colour. With this design, you should keep the flowers at equal distances from one another. To do this, first find the central spiral by holding the cone in your left hand, and with a felt pen, make a slanting line at the top. Measure 7·5 cm (3 in) from this line to the centre of the cone and make another felt pen mark. Make another mark 7·5 cm (3 in) below this. Join these three marks with a slanting line drawn and insert the first row of flowers on this line. You can then work backwards from this line filling in the design.

Below: Pyramid or cone-shaped arrangements can be made in any size, but bear in mind that they use a considerable amount of dried plant material.

Small cone

Make the cone (see opposite) and attach it to the base. Collect together all the material you want to use; it must all be wired and you will need more material than you might think! In this sort of arrangement, the material is very tightly packed and arranged in very concentrated fashion. Be sure you have enough; it is infuriating to run out with your cone only half finished.

The cone in the picture was made with the following material: small helichrysum flowers, acorns in their cups, small poppy seed heads, tiny fir cones, tiny clumps of yarrow, box leaves, helipterum and opened beech masts.

The easiest way to work a cone is to divide it into four quarters and begin by positioning the material down the four vertical lines. Then start filling in from the bottom, using the larger material first and grading it as you progress up the cone. Aim to get spots of deep colour strategically positioned around and up the cone. In this instance, these are provided by the dark red helichrysum flowers.

The other way to work a cone is to start at the bottom, pushing the material in all around and then continue working upwards in ever decreasing circles until you reach the top. This is a good way to work if you are planning a cone which has definite circular layers of similar flowers or seed heads. The one pictured has a more random type of design, which nevertheless must 'work' visually. Apart from the spots of colour, some of the material is still slightly recessed to give an uneven surface. Considerable care has been given to the top of the cone, which is beautifully designed with a cluster of seed heads. After all, this is the focal point of this kind of arrangement, so do make sure it is truly a 'crowning glory'.

When you have finished the cone, go over it again filling in with tiny bits of material to make sure there are no gaps anywhere. It really must be tightly packed. Keep turning the cone round so you can see how it looks from all angles. Then stand away a little and see how it looks from a distance.

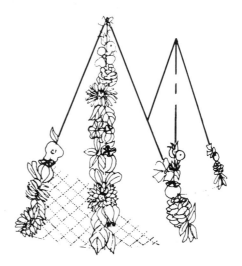

There are two ways of working a cone arrangement. Above: Position material down the quarter lines and then fill in between them. Below: Working upwards from the base, position material closely all around the cone.

Arrangement on pegboard, bark or wood
The natural colours and textures of bark or wood have a beauty of their own and make an excellent foil for preserved flowers and foliage. However, such an item is not always easy to acquire, whereas pegboard (which is easy to obtain), can be just as effective.

First secure a piece of dry foam or styrofoam on to the board. Do this by crossing wires over the top of the foam, then inserting them through the holes in the board and twisting them together, on top of the foam. This means they are less likely to scratch either the wall (if the arrangement is to be hung) or the table (if it is to stand on one). As a further precaution, however, stick a piece of felt or similar material over the wires on the base of the pegboard or bark.

If you are using white pegboard, give it a coating of brown or dark green paint, but make sure that your arrangement covers the pegboard completely.

If you are using bark or a 'slice' of wood as a base, fix the foam to the base by putting three or four small pieces of Blu-tack on to the foam. Press in place on the bark, giving it a little twist, to make it firm.

This type of base can now be used to work an all-round, diagonal or oblong arrangement. Although, as already mentioned, an arrangement on pegboard is more attractive if the board is covered by the material, this does not necessarily apply if using a piece of wood or bark. If this is attractively marked or coloured, it can form an integral part of the design. The arrangement can either be hung on a wall or used as a window ledge or table arrangement. For hanging, fix a staple to the back of the wood or bark, or make a loop with fine wire and insert through pegboard.

Below: A pegboard-based arrangement.

Arrangement on pegboard

This beautiful arrangement is another of those versatile ones that can be hung or put on a table, chest, sideboard or whatever. In fact, it would look lovely as a central decoration at a winter dinner party, and it is sufficiently low not to interfere with vision and conversation across the table. It is composed of beech leaves, small cones, box leaves, tiny holly leaves, *Garrya elliptica*, honesty pods and helichrysum flowers. The beautiful focal point 'flowers' are made with honesty seed pods that have been stuck into the cones. The particularly attractive feature of them, however, is that the honesty pods were picked while still quite young, so they have retained a marvellous, delicate purple colour.

A small piece of foam was wired to the centre of a piece of pegboard to provide the support for the material, then the outer length extremities of the design were established with beech leaves. The narrower width of the design was established next, also with beech leaves.

The focal point of the cone and honesty 'flowers' was then positioned; the largest one is in the centre of the design. Note how the other large one has been placed at a very definite angle, pointing outwards away from the main one. The cones were positioned next at opposite corners of the arrangement. In one corner a single large cone was used, while opposite it, there is a little spray of three small ones. This illustrates again the importance of *balance* as opposed to perfect symmetry. Finally the design was filled in and completed with the remaining material, working from the centre out to the edge. You will see how the helichrysum flowers provide strategic splashes of colour and are placed at varying angles throughout the arrangement.

Below: For a low, flat-based arrangement, wire foam to pegboard (left). Below, foam has been glued to an interesting piece of wood, which makes an attractive vehicle for an arrangement.

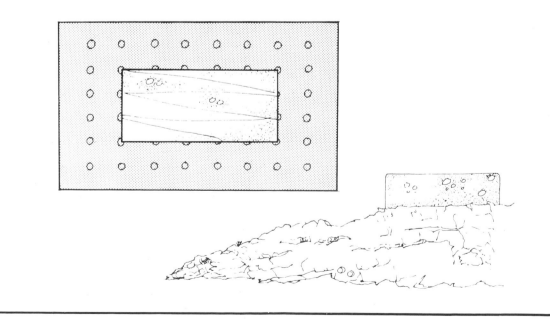

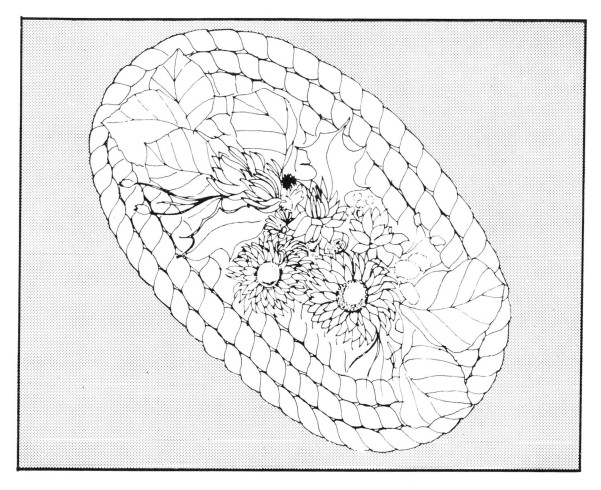

Design worked on rush mat or flat wicker-work tray

A rush mat or wickerwork tray makes a most attractive base or background for a dried arrangement as the 'natural' texture of the rushes or cane offsets the subtle colours of dried plant material to perfection. If there is a decorative border to the mat or tray, in-corporate it into the design, making the best use of it to complement your arrangement.

If you want to hang the final arrangement, push a length of wire through the weave at the centre top and twist it into a loop at the back of the mat. Then secure a piece of dried foam to the centre with a piece of wire in the same way as for a pegboard arrangement. Protect the back in a similar way too.

You will need a selection of wired leaves, flowers and seed heads for such a design. You could, in fact, just push the wires through the wickerwork, but you will have to protect

Above: When using a rush or canework mat as a base for an arrangement, the dried plant material should first be wired. It can then be carefully pushed through the canework to form the design. Cover the back with a piece of thick felt to prevent the wall or table surface from being scratched.

the whole area at the back with a large piece of felt if you do so. Begin the arrange-ment at the edge of the shape you have planned, and work in towards the centre. Beech leaves, or something similar, make a good border for such a design and help to establish a definite outline. If these are not wired individually, you can attach them by holding the stem against the mat with your thumb and putting a short piece of wire across the stem. Push the ends of this through the weave and twist the ends together at the back. Clip them off close to the matting.

Design on a circular canework tray

The base of this extremely attractive design is an inexpensive canework tray, available from most craft-type shops. A charming design has been worked in it with material carefully chosen to complement the natural colour of the cane.

As you can see, the design worked is triangular and, in general, it is more usual not to work a circular design on a circular tray or mat. If you did work a circular design, it would be important that it was perfectly positioned and perfectly round, which is really quite difficult to achieve.

The material, which comprises beech leaves, cotoneaster, a magnolia leaf, ornamental grasses, helichrysum flowers, hydrangea petals and ballota is pushed into a small piece of foam which has been wired on to the centre of the basket. A small hook made of twisted wire was also put on the back for hanging the tray on a wall.

First the triangular outline was established with beech leaves and cotoneaster, after which the design was filled in, working towards the centre all the time. The focal point here is the dark magnolia leaf which has been placed slightly to the left of the centre. It is more attractive with this sort of arrangement to put the focal point slightly off centre, so you do not have perfect symmetry. This is particularly applicable when the outline is a little irregular, as it is here.

Rush, wicker and canework bases look better hung on a dark background, as this tends to throw up the colours both of the base and of the dried material used in the design.

Japanese fan design

This is a lovely example of using an unusual background for a design of dried plant material. This arrangement of beech leaves, corn sheath flowers, yarrow, statice and golden rod has been worked on a Japanese fan – again inexpensive but amazingly effective.

A small piece of foam was wired to the fan close to the handle and the design worked by beginning with an outline of beech leaves. Obviously, the shape of the design is dictated by the fan here, but this one has been cleverly worked so that it looks equally effective whether you hang it with the handle at the top or the bottom. The design has been taken downwards over the handle, so that it really 'works' in all directions.

An arrangement in a jar or clear gift box

These arrangements make very attractive gifts, and are particularly useful in kitchens

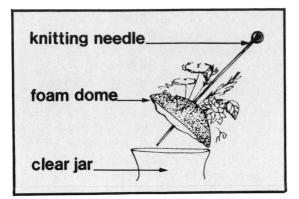

knitting needle

foam dome

clear jar

Above: The knitting needle is placed in the centre of the foam ball, taking care not to disturb the flowers and foliage which have been arranged. It is then lowered into the glass jar to complete the arrangement (see bottom).

or bathrooms, where an arrangement is likely to suffer from steam. For such an arrangement, you need:

☐ Glass jar or box (make sure it is quite clean inside)
☐ Plasticine or Blu-tack
☐ Half a plastic foam ball
☐ Dried leaves and grasses
☐ Wired flowers and buds
☐ Clear adhesive tape

Measure the glass, so you know the maximum size you can make your arrangement. Remember to keep within these confines! Begin the arrangement by inserting a long-stemmed flower or seed head in the centre of the foam dome. From there work outwards, adding shorter-stemmed leaves and flowers all round. Do not make the arrangement so large that it will overcrowd the jar, but try to make certain that the material covers the foam base, so that none of it shows through the arrangement.

To place the arrangement in a jar, put a piece of Plasticine or Blu-tack on the base of foam, then push a skewer or knitting needle down the centre, taking care not to disturb the arrangement. Lower it slowly into the jar, giving it a slight twist to make certain that the Plasticine or Blu-tack sticks to the glass. Put the lid of the jar in place, and if necessary, secure it with a little clear tape. Polish the outside with a soft cloth.

If using a clear gift box, secure the piece of foam in the same way to the inside base of the box and seal the lid with a strip of clear tape all round.

A very quick and easy flower decoration can be made by filling a glass jar with the heads of flowers, and it is a good way of using up any odds and ends of short-stemmed flowers. Put a cardboard tube, cut to the same height as the jar, inside it, leaving room for the flowers between it and the sides of the jar. Secure the tube in position with a little Plasticine or Blu-tack. Then fill the jar with flowers, facing them outwards in the jar, and making sure you do not squash them. (A pair of tweezers are a help when placing the flower heads in position.) Helichrysum in varying shades are particularly effective.

Other creative ideas

Personalized greeting cards and gift tags made with flowers, leaves and grasses you have dried yourself are always appreciated. Card can be bought from most stationers and art shops, in a variety of colours, but remember that the plain backs of old Christmas and birthday cards are infinitely useful (and cheap!). If possible, use card with a matt or dull finish, as dried material does not always stick too well to a gloss finish.

The size and shape of a card or gift tag is, of course, a matter of personal choice, but for tags it is advisable to keep to a measurement of between 5–7·5 cm (2–3 in) overall. Make a hole for the cord with a pointed skewer or needle as neatly as possible. For greetings cards, a good average size is 12·5 × 10 cm (5 × 4 in) and to make this you need a piece of card 12·5 × 20 cm (5 × 8 in). Find the centre,

score a line along it with a knife on the inside of the card, and fold over. If you want to make a rectangular card, cut a piece of card 27·5 × 10 cm (11 × 4 in), measure 6·5 cm (2¾ in) in from the outside edges, score on the inside and fold this towards the centre.

When decorating these cards or tags, use small flowers, leaves or berries and make the design follow the line of the card. Use tweezers for the small and delicate material and as little adhesive as possible to secure it in place. Make sure the material is always of a size proportionate to the card or tag.

Below: Small dried flowers can be used to make pretty, personalized greetings cards or gift tags. They can also be used to make your own wrapping paper for an extra-special gift (not shown).

Bookmarkers and place name-tags

These are very quick and easy to make, but most effective. You will need:

- ☐ Lengths of ribbon, silk or velvet
- ☐ Small dried flowers and foliage
- ☐ Masking tape or iron-on vilene. (Masking tape can be bought at most do-it-yourself shops, stationers and ironmongers.)

Cut a length of ribbon 30 cm (12 in) long, and shape one end by cutting it diagonally. Cut a piece of masking tape 20 cm (8 in) long, and stick to the back of the ribbon, allowing approximately 5 cm (2 in) for turning at the top. (Alternatively cut a piece of vilene to the same length and iron it on to the back of the ribbon.) Secure the turning with a staple or dab of glue, and glue one or two flowers and leaves at this end of the ribbon to cover.

Any width of ribbon may be used for bookmarkers and place name-tags. The tape or vilene used as backing should stop just short of the edges. If the ribbon is considerably wider than the tape or vilene, stick two strips down the back, allowing one to slightly overlap the other. If you are using these as name-tags, attach the name card just under the flowers with a dab of glue.

You could also make 'stand-up' place name-cards for a special dinner party by cutting pieces of strong card 7·5 × 5 cm (3 × 2 in), scoring a line lengthwise down the centre and folding in half. Write the name of your guests on each one and, if you like, stick a different coloured flower or seed head on the side of each.

Below: A dried flower bookmark.

Insert: Your guests will feel truly welcome with their own place-name card.

Pictures and plaques

Above: An old fashioned oval frame sets off this beautiful design to perfection.

When making a picture, whether it is a 'hanging' on a background of linen or other material, a plaque or a framed design, there are a few general principles it is wise to bear in mind. Always choose the background material carefully, to blend in with the material you will be using and remember, too, that eventually, even when hung on a sunless wall, the natural colours will fade a little.

If, like most of us, ideas for pictures and designs do not come to you naturally and easily, even when, or perhaps particularly when, you have a pile of dried material in front of you, don't worry — just look around. Ideas for designs are everywhere — on post-cards, birthday cards, patterned fabrics, pieces of china and so on. Be prepared — and quite shameless — to copy and use them to your advantage!

Do not overcrowd your picture; place large

Above and left: Convex-shaped glass has been used so as not to flatten the design.

flowers, seed heads and the stronger col-oured material to the centre of the design, taking the smaller buds and more delicate material to the outside. Try to make the flowers and leaves look as if they are growing, by using their natural curves, unless you have decided on a symmetrical design.

When making a symmetrical design, inci-dentally, it helps if you measure the backing

accurately to find the centre and halfway points; then dot the material with pins or a pencil at the points where you want to place the main items.

It is always wise to experiment with the design and material before gluing it down, moving things around until you find the most pleasing combination. Rubber-based adhesives are the best to use as they rub easily off the fingers and most materials; whatever glue you use, however, the prime rule is *use it sparingly*.

Skeletonized leaves are particularly effec-tive when used in a framed picture. Choose a darker colour as background material in this instance as it will throw the tracery of veins into relief. Incidentally, never hang pictures or arrangements of dried flowers in direct, strong sunlight; it will make the colours fade too quickly.

Hanging 'picture'
For this you will need:

☐ Thin card
☐ Linen or similar textured material for background
☐ Length of dowelling rod

☐ Adhesive
☐ Dried flowers, foliage etc. (unwired)
☐ Braid for edges (optional)

For a square picture measuring approximately 25 × 20 cm (10 × 8 in) you will need a piece of linen or background fabric measuring 30 × 23 cm (12 × 9 in). If it is at all creased, press it with a warm iron. Cut a piece of card 25 × 20 cm (10 × 8 in), put spots of glue along the edges and across the centre and place it on the linen near to the bottom, allowing approximately 1 cm ($\frac{1}{2}$ in) for turning. This then gives a larger turning at the top to go over the piece of dowelling rod. Cut a length of dowelling about 30 cm (12 in) long and put this at the top of the card, against the linen. Turn the raw edges of the linen to the back of the card and glue down, checking first that the dowelling rod is quite straight. When the glue has dried, neaten the back by gluing another piece of card over raw edges.

The 'hanging' is now ready for decorating, and the designs you can work are innumerable! Experiment by placing material in position, moving it around and trying different combinations of colour. You may find it helpful to attach the 'hanging' to a pastry board or similar board with a few pieces of adhesive tape to give you a firm base upon which to work. Do remember to use the glue sparingly when you come to actually fix the material in place. If you like, silk cord or braid can be.glued around the edges of the completed hanging to form an 'informal frame'.

Small picture on green hessian
This is the easiest picture of all to do. The base is an old table mat which has been covered with green hessian stuck down firmly on the back of the board with wide masking tape. A couple of hooks have been screwed in for hanging.

The design has been worked from varied seed heads, helichrysum flowers, senecio, tiny poppy seed heads and leaves. Note, too, the unusual tiny piece of 'curled' wood that has been slotted into the right of the picture. Whilst it completely fits into the design, it provides an added bit of interest in the overall effect.

The whole design of this sort of picture should always be worked out to your complete satisfaction before gluing anything in place. You certainly do not want to start moving material around once it has been glued, or you will get an awful mess on the background fabric, which will be hard to remove. Start by establishing the outline; in this case it is a triangular shape which has been created by the dark leaves. Work from the outside of the design towards the centre, so that the central material will be the last to be glued in position and thus will be 'raised' above the rest.

When you come to gluing, do use the absolute minimum amount of adhesive, but make sure everything is secure. If you like you could add a braid border to the edge of the mat.

Picture on brown dralon

This picture has been worked in a bought frame. (It could easily have been made at home.) The backing was removed and covered in dralon and then fixed back in position on the frame. Incidentally, a dull finish material is better than one with a shiny or satin finish as it tends to show off this 'natural' material better.

This picture was worked with a selection of box leaves, laurel leaves, beech leaves, individual bells of Ireland, acorns in their cups, tiny cones, helichrysum flowers, iris seed heads, poppy seed heads and open beech masts. It is a formal, bold design, with the bright colour cleverly kept to a clump in the centre, so that your eye is drawn there. As the material throughout the design is clustered in a concentrated fashion, the contrast of textures and shapes needs careful consideration.

The design was worked following exactly the same principles as those in the small picture on the table mat – that is, the outline was established first and the design then worked into the centre. Again, nothing was glued in position until the design was satisfactory.

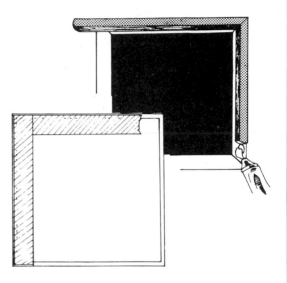

Above: Use glue sparingly when fixing the covered backing to the frame.

Framed picture on green hessian

This is a rather more delicate and slightly less formal picture, that would be suitable for hanging in a bedroom. The design is balanced rather than symmetrical, and gives a feeling of greater movement than the more rigid design of the picture. Note how instead of a cluster of strong colour in the centre, this picture has a diagonal line of colour leading down to the right of the design.

It was again worked on the same lines as the previous one and is composed of grasses, acorns in their cups, poppy seed heads, box, hydrangea petals and various other seed heads.

Right: This picture would look delightful on a contrasting-coloured wall.

Making a plaque

For this, you will need:

- [ ] Plywood
- [ ] Glue
- [ ] Rubber adhesive
- [ ] Velvet braid
- [ ] Dried material

These are usually oval or oblong, but the shape and size are again a highly individual choice, and will often be governed by where the plaque is to hang. The lightest and easiest material to use is plywood, preferably 6 or 8 mm ($\frac{1}{4}$ or $\frac{1}{3}$ in) thick. Many do-it-yourself shops have offcuts of suitable material, and if you ask they will cut them to the size you want.

Decide on the backing material you want to use – it could be velvet, hessian, felt, slub silk or coloured corduroy, for example. Choose a colour to fit in with the colour scheme in the room where the plaque is to hang. Stretch the backing material over the piece of plywood, using a few pins to hold it in place, then stick the raw edges down on the back of plywood using rubber adhesive. Attach a screw or staple on the back for hanging. (If necessary, do this before sticking down the backing material.)

Glue braid carefully round the edge before beginning the design. Then assemble the dried material – flowers, foliage, seed heads, perhaps a few tiny shells. Once again experiment with the design by placing material in various positions, following any natural curves as far as possible. Having decided on the design and colour scheme place a 'marker', such as a long piece of grass, in the centre, and then work the design from the outside edge in towards the centre. You may not necessarily use the 'marker' in the actual design, but it helps when trying to achieve a balanced, symmetrical design.

Plaques can be easily transformed into a framed picture by omitting the braid, and sticking a lightweight beading or picture 'edging' round the outside, mitring the corners carefully.

Right: An attractive trimming in toning colours adds the finishing touch.

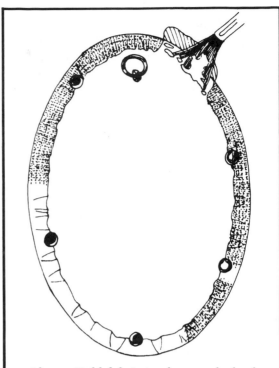

Above: Hold fabric in place on the back of the plaque with pins while gluing it.

Framing a mirror

A very ordinary cheap mirror from a chain store can be transformed into an *object d'art* by adding a border of dried flowers. This may either be glued to the frame itself, or positioned just inside the frame on the glass, so that the dried material partly covers the frame. If the mirror is unframed, stick braid round the edge, and then add dried material to harmonize with the colours of the braid.

When working on a shiny surface, such as a mirror, use a contact adhesive which dries very quickly. Work your design out on paper first so you can work quickly and definitely once you start on the actual mirror. Any glue which may fall on the mirror can be removed with turpentine.

Your design may be symmetrical, with flower heads interspersed at regular intervals with small sprigs of foliage and leaves, or you could have a focal point at the top corner of the mirror and curve sprays of flowers/foliage away from this point.

Below: Make sure the design does not obscure the whole surface of the mirror. Note how the flower at the bottom left has been positioned to hide the join in the trim.